6 —

Crystal: The Story of a Real Baby Whale

Crystal: The Story of a Real Baby Whale

By Karen C. Smyth

Illustrated by Norma Cuneo

ISBN 0-89272-223-1
Library of Congress Catalog Card Number 85-52440

Composition by Typeworks, Belfast, Maine
Manufactured at Courier Stoughton, Inc., Stoughton, Mass.

10   9   8   7   6   5

DOWN EAST BOOKS / Camden, Maine

To Ibis,
who now swims free—
as is every whale's natural right

The characters in this story are real whales.

WINTER

In early January, many places in the world have snow on the ground, and the water is cold and frozen into ice. But in the southern part of the North Atlantic Ocean there is a place where it never snows or freezes, and there is summer weather all year round.

And here a humpback whale is born.

Bright sun rays slanting in the warm, clear, sound-filled water greet the baby whale, whose name is Crystal. For nearly a year he grew inside his mother, and now he is suddenly free, as if in an endless bathtub. Gently Salt, his mother, pushes him to the surface to take his first breath.

Inhale—and *whoosh*, a misty little exhale! A new whale's life begins.

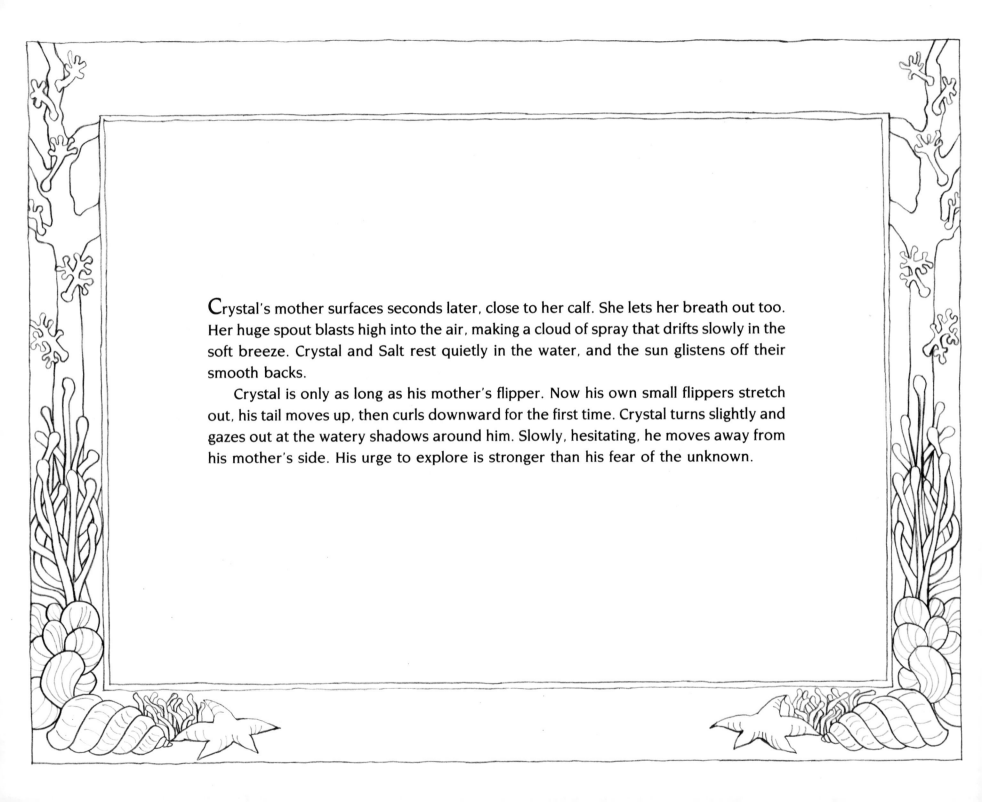

Crystal's mother surfaces seconds later, close to her calf. She lets her breath out too. Her huge spout blasts high into the air, making a cloud of spray that drifts slowly in the soft breeze. Crystal and Salt rest quietly in the water, and the sun glistens off their smooth backs.

Crystal is only as long as his mother's flipper. Now his own small flippers stretch out, his tail moves up, then curls downward for the first time. Crystal turns slightly and gazes out at the watery shadows around him. Slowly, hesitating, he moves away from his mother's side. His urge to explore is stronger than his fear of the unknown.

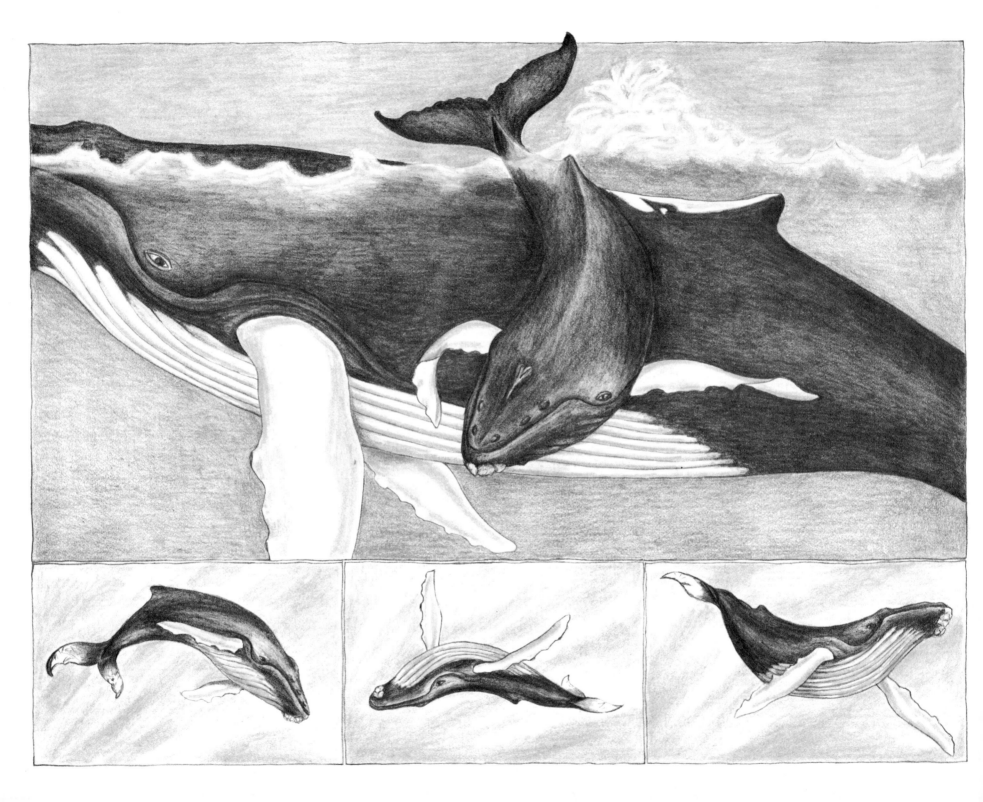

Though he is only a few moments old, Crystal needs no help from Salt as he begins to dip and splash about. He's awkward at first as he moves one of his flippers, then the other, then both together, trying to steer and keep his balance. His little tail tips forward and breaks the surface, splashing his mother's side. Crystal is clumsy as he rolls, dives, and turns, learning to swim by moving his flippers and tail. It is all so new—and there is *so* much water!

But Crystal stays close to his mother. Often he passes underneath her, surfacing by her tail, and sometimes near her head. His mother hangs in the water, watchful and calm. Occasionally she reaches out with her flipper to softly brush Crystal's side as he swims around her. Finally she gives a loud, rumbling spout, arches her broad back, and dives down several feet beneath the surface. Crystal spouts twice and follows her.

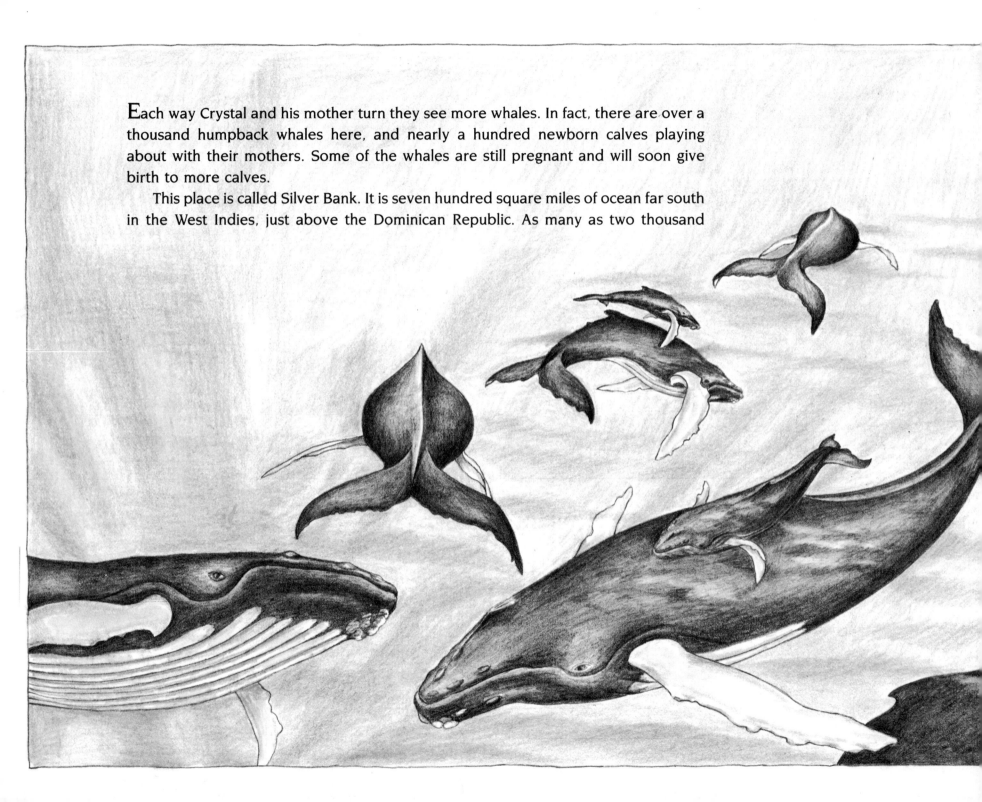

Each way Crystal and his mother turn they see more whales. In fact, there are over a thousand humpback whales here, and nearly a hundred newborn calves playing about with their mothers. Some of the whales are still pregnant and will soon give birth to more calves.

This place is called Silver Bank. It is seven hundred square miles of ocean far south in the West Indies, just above the Dominican Republic. As many as two thousand

humpback whales come here each winter to have their babies and to mate, because the water is shallow and warm. Silver Bank is far from land and undisturbed by boats. The water temperature is about eighty degrees—as warm as the air on a hot summer day—even in the middle of winter! On the sandy bottom is a colorful garden of corals, sea fans, and anemones.

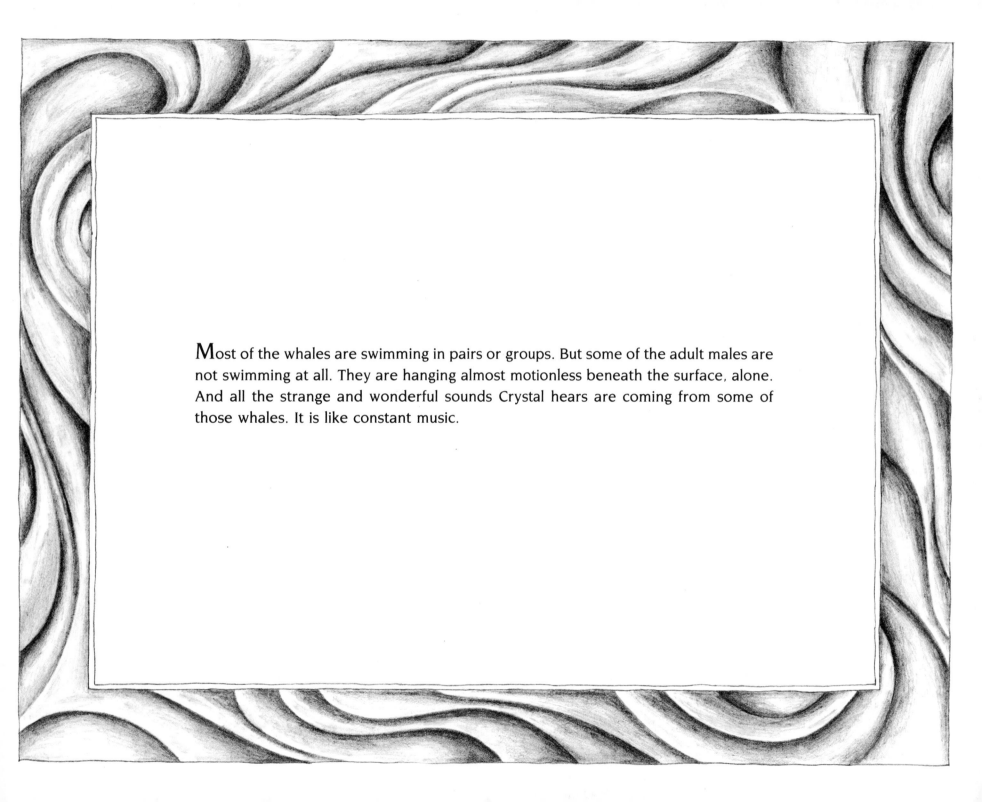

Most of the whales are swimming in pairs or groups. But some of the adult males are not swimming at all. They are hanging almost motionless beneath the surface, alone. And all the strange and wonderful sounds Crystal hears are coming from some of those whales. It is like constant music.

Crystal is no small baby. At birth he is nearly thirteen feet long (longer than *two* grown men!).

And he weighs over a thousand pounds—as much as a small car!

To go forward, Crystal only has to move his tail up and down. The flukes at the end of his tail are like a giant paddle. Fish swim by moving their tails from side to side, but whales are not fish. All whales are mammals, just like horses, dogs, elephants, and people. They are all warm-blooded and they breathe air. They give birth to live babies, and nurse their babies. Millions of years ago the ancestors of whales lived on land, like other mammals. Now whales spend their whole lives swimming, playing, eating, even sleeping in the water. Whales are the largest animals ever to have lived on Earth. Crystal's mother weighs more than six elephants!

Some parts of the whales' bodies have changed to make life easier in the ocean. The front legs have become flippers (pectoral fins) and the rear legs have disappeared. The nose is now on top of the head, and the nostrils are called a blowhole. It takes a whale only a few seconds to exhale and inhale because it doesn't have to lift its whole head out of the water. Whales breathe very deeply and they exchange almost all the air in their lungs in a single breath. This means they don't have to breathe as often as people, and can stay beneath the surface longer before having to come up for air.

You can see a whale's blow, or spout. As the whale exhales, the warm air from its lungs mixes with oils and moisture in the blowhole and with surrounding seawater to make a spray. On a clear day with very little wind you can see the blow of a whale from over a mile away!

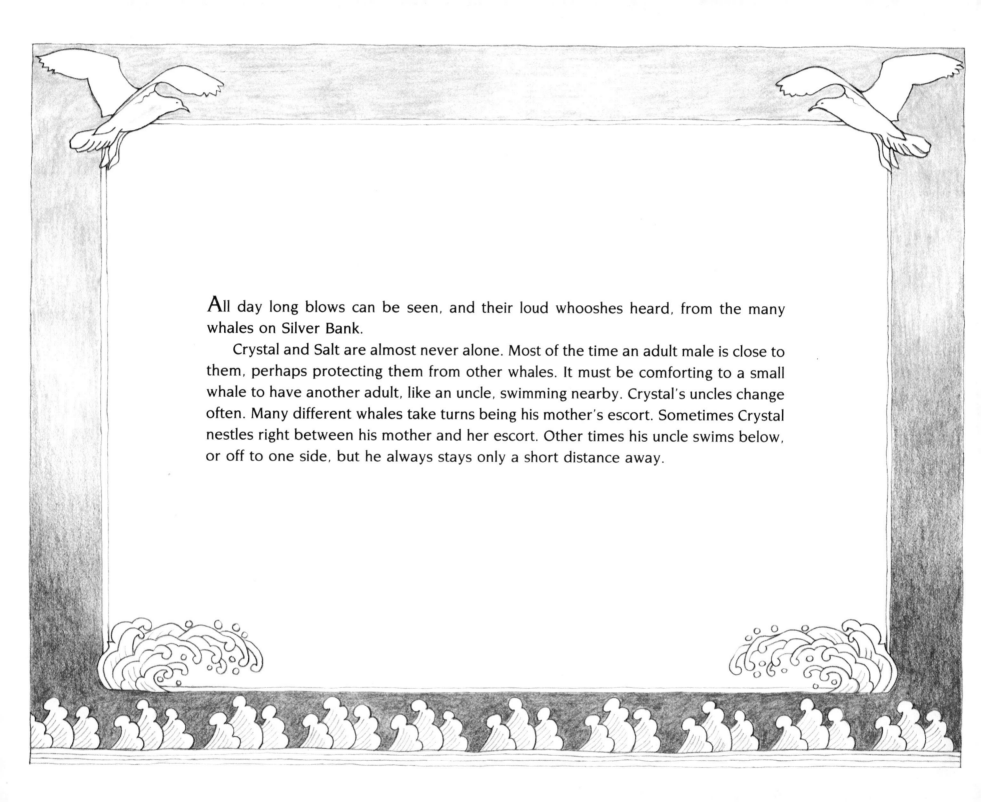

All day long blows can be seen, and their loud whooshes heard, from the many whales on Silver Bank.

Crystal and Salt are almost never alone. Most of the time an adult male is close to them, perhaps protecting them from other whales. It must be comforting to a small whale to have another adult, like an uncle, swimming nearby. Crystal's uncles change often. Many different whales take turns being his mother's escort. Sometimes Crystal nestles right between his mother and her escort. Other times his uncle swims below, or off to one side, but he always stays only a short distance away.

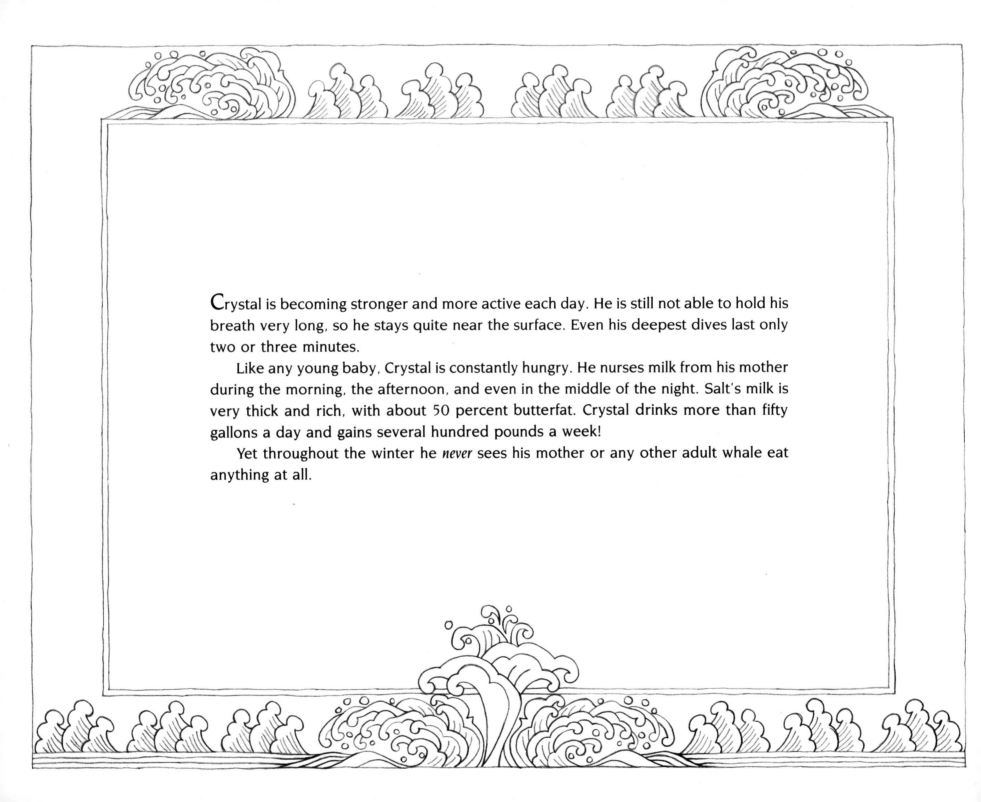

Crystal is becoming stronger and more active each day. He is still not able to hold his breath very long, so he stays quite near the surface. Even his deepest dives last only two or three minutes.

Like any young baby, Crystal is constantly hungry. He nurses milk from his mother during the morning, the afternoon, and even in the middle of the night. Salt's milk is very thick and rich, with about 50 percent butterfat. Crystal drinks more than fifty gallons a day and gains several hundred pounds a week!

Yet throughout the winter he *never* sees his mother or any other adult whale eat anything at all.

Instead he watches a lot of rough-housing among the adults. Often the males compete with one another for a female's attention. Sometimes it seems like friendly play, but once in a while it is quite wild and rowdy, with lots of splashing. Several times Crystal and his mother find themselves in a group of as many as ten whales, all slapping their strong tails and flippers, rolling and snorting loudly. The air around them fills with white spray! Occasionally Crystal is bumped and even whacked accidentally by flying flippers. It must be most confusing for a young calf, but perhaps very exciting too!

As the weeks pass Crystal begins to imitate some of the older whales. He finds that while he is lying on his side he too can raise his long flipper high into the air, wave it, and sometimes slap it down in the water. This is called flippering. A loud splash of his own now joins the confusion of splashing sounds made by the others all around him. Crystal often rolls over completely on his back and brings *both* flippers high in the air.

Hours and hours pass as Crystal plays, flippering and even jumping partway out of the water. Sometimes he bounces off his mother's or uncle's side or lands on their backs. Making the jump is easier than planning *where* he will land!

Only humpback whales have such long white flippers. The Latin name for humpbacks is *Megaptera novaeangliae*, which means "big-winged New Englander." An adult's wing-like flippers can be as long as fifteen feet. The flippers are another part of the whale that is similar to land mammals. Inside Crystal's flipper are bones almost exactly like those in a human arm, even finger bones!

Like arms, Crystal's flippers are flexible. He can move them separately or together to steer. He can even swim backward! As they swim beneath the surface, humpbacks can turn, bend, and roll as if in slow motion, as graceful as birds in flight.

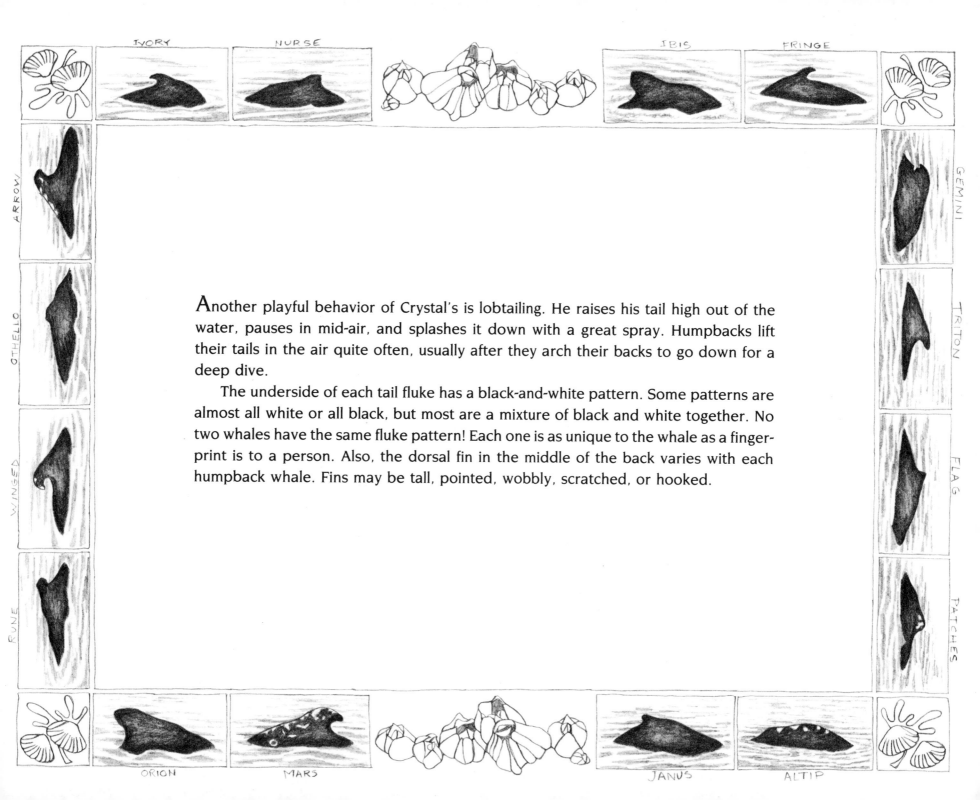

Another playful behavior of Crystal's is lobtailing. He raises his tail high out of the water, pauses in mid-air, and splashes it down with a great spray. Humpbacks lift their tails in the air quite often, usually after they arch their backs to go down for a deep dive.

The underside of each tail fluke has a black-and-white pattern. Some patterns are almost all white or all black, but most are a mixture of black and white together. No two whales have the same fluke pattern! Each one is as unique to the whale as a fingerprint is to a person. Also, the dorsal fin in the middle of the back varies with each humpback whale. Fins may be tall, pointed, wobbly, scratched, or hooked.

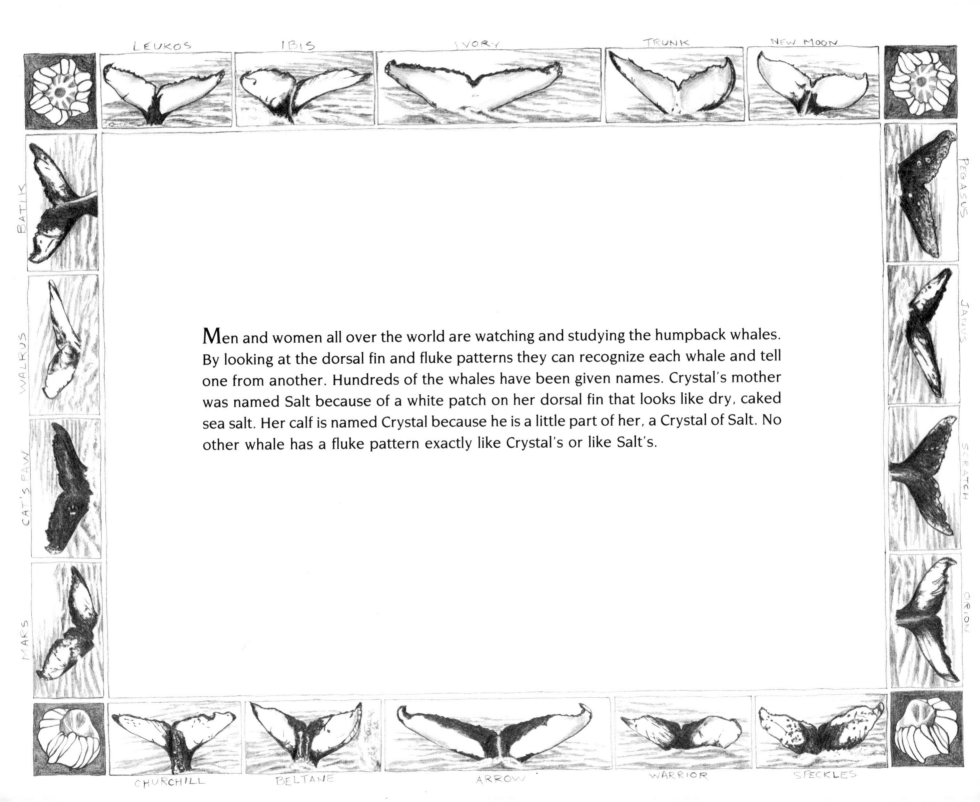

Men and women all over the world are watching and studying the humpback whales. By looking at the dorsal fin and fluke patterns they can recognize each whale and tell one from another. Hundreds of the whales have been given names. Crystal's mother was named Salt because of a white patch on her dorsal fin that looks like dry, caked sea salt. Her calf is named Crystal because he is a little part of her, a Crystal of Salt. No other whale has a fluke pattern exactly like Crystal's or like Salt's.

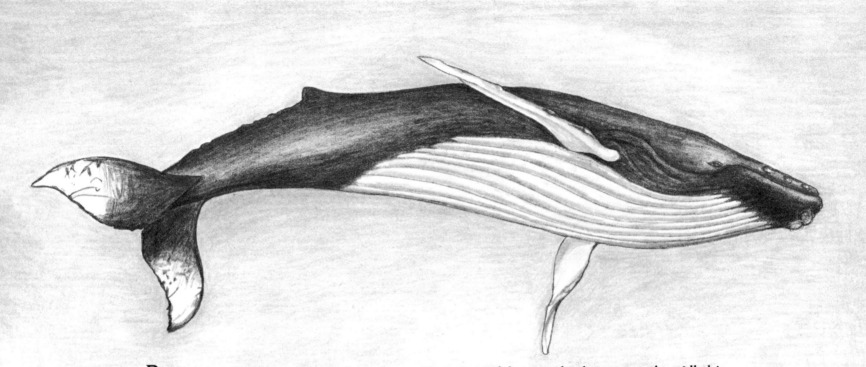

By the end of March, Salt has been nursing Crystal for nearly three months. All this time Crystal has been growing rapidly. He is now about four feet longer, and has gained several thousand pounds! Salt, however, is *very* hungry. There is almost no food in these warm waters, and she has not eaten all winter!

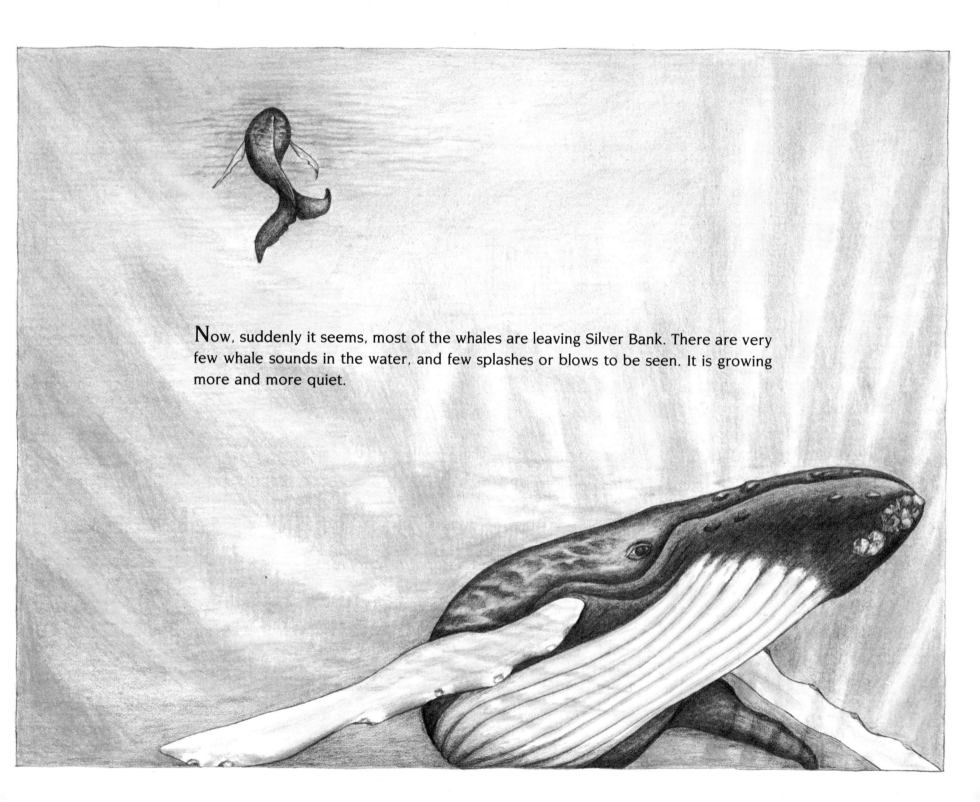

Now, suddenly it seems, most of the whales are leaving Silver Bank. There are very few whale sounds in the water, and few splashes or blows to be seen. It is growing more and more quiet.

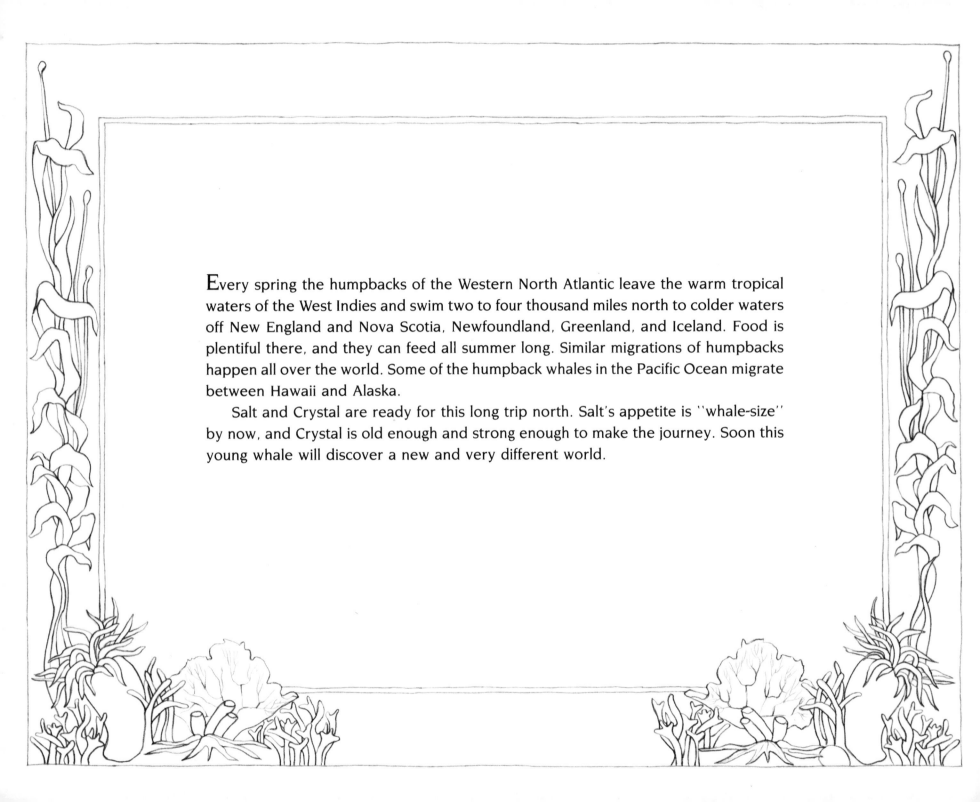

Every spring the humpbacks of the Western North Atlantic leave the warm tropical waters of the West Indies and swim two to four thousand miles north to colder waters off New England and Nova Scotia, Newfoundland, Greenland, and Iceland. Food is plentiful there, and they can feed all summer long. Similar migrations of humpbacks happen all over the world. Some of the humpback whales in the Pacific Ocean migrate between Hawaii and Alaska.

Salt and Crystal are ready for this long trip north. Salt's appetite is "whale-size" by now, and Crystal is old enough and strong enough to make the journey. Soon this young whale will discover a new and very different world.

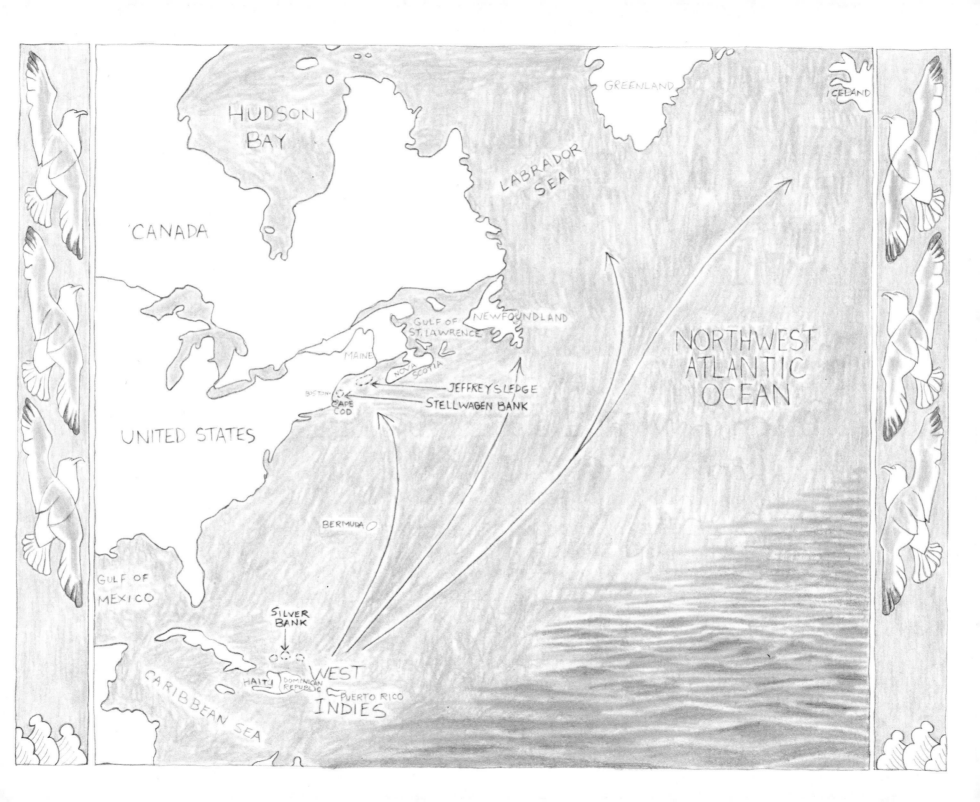

SPRING

The weeks pass in the vast sea. Salt and Crystal swim, then rest, day and night. How do they sleep? Whales can't lie on the ocean bottom because they have to keep breathing air. So when they rest, Crystal and Salt float at the surface of the water, hardly moving at all. This is called logging because from a distance they look like floating logs, drifting quietly.

As they swim north the water becomes cooler and cooler. There is no time for play now in this long journey. Once in a while Crystal sees a few other whales in the distance, but usually he and Salt are all by themselves. How do the humpbacks navigate? How do Salt and Crystal know where to go each day as they find their way to their northern feeding grounds? Their travel surely follows some kind of pattern. Perhaps they use the sun, moon, or stars for guides. Maybe underwater canyons and mountains are the landmarks for these paths known only to the whales.

By early May, Salt and Crystal have been traveling north for nearly one and a half months. They have covered nearly two thousand miles! Finally they pass Cape Cod, Massachusetts, and arrive at the edge of Stellwagen Bank. The water here is much colder than at Silver Bank—only about fifty-five degrees.

All "banks," like Silver and Stellwagen, are shoals—shallow places in the ocean. Stellwagen is sometimes called Middle Bank because this sandy shoal stretches twenty-six miles between Cape Ann and Cape Cod. Under the water, the bank is as high as an eleven-story building! When the ocean currents hit the steep sides of this bank the water is pushed up toward the surface. This causes a tremendous upwelling of rich nutrients from the ocean bottom. Sunlight penetrates the upper layer of seawater and gives the energy needed for an enormous variety of plants to grow. All this vegetable food makes Stellwagen a rich breeding and feeding ground for all types of fish: cod, flounder, herring, bluefish, haddock, tuna, and more. So Stellwagen is a *busy* place, with lots of fish and many different kinds of fishing boats—draggers, seiners, gill-netters, and sports fishermen.

Humpback whales feed on different kinds of fish, depending on where they live. Humpbacks always look for *little* fish. They do not have teeth, so they can't chew, and their throats are very small. They eat herring, capelin, squid, small cod, and even shrimp. One of their favorite foods on Stellwagen Bank is a fish that looks like a little snake, only six or seven inches long, called a sand lance (or sand eel). These fish swim in huge groups, called schools, and probably got their name because at night they swim down to the bottom and bury themselves in the sand.

When Crystal first sees sand eels, he watches not one, but thousands! They look like a thick cloud in the water, but the cloud changes shape and moves very quickly!

Crystal must be fascinated by these swarms of tiny fish but he never gets close. Even swimming as fast as he can, he has a hard time catching up to them.

It isn't long before Crystal sees his hungry mother go after those eels and catch a lot of them. She is finally feeding for the first time in months. Crystal has never seen Salt swim so fast. Her powerful tail slashes in the water as she plunges, with her mouth open, right through the middle of a school of sand eels! Her throat expands like a balloon, making a huge pouch filled with water and hundreds of fish. Quickly she closes her mouth and the ''balloon'' shrinks, forcing the seawater out before she swallows the fish.

Like all humpback whales, Salt has several deep folds in her skin—like pleats on the underside of her body—running all the way from her chin to her mid-belly. The pleats expand and contract when she is feeding so she can get more fish in each mouthful. And, like any other mammal, whales cannot drink much of the salty ocean water, which is why they push it out of their mouths as they feed. They get most of their liquids from their food during digestion.

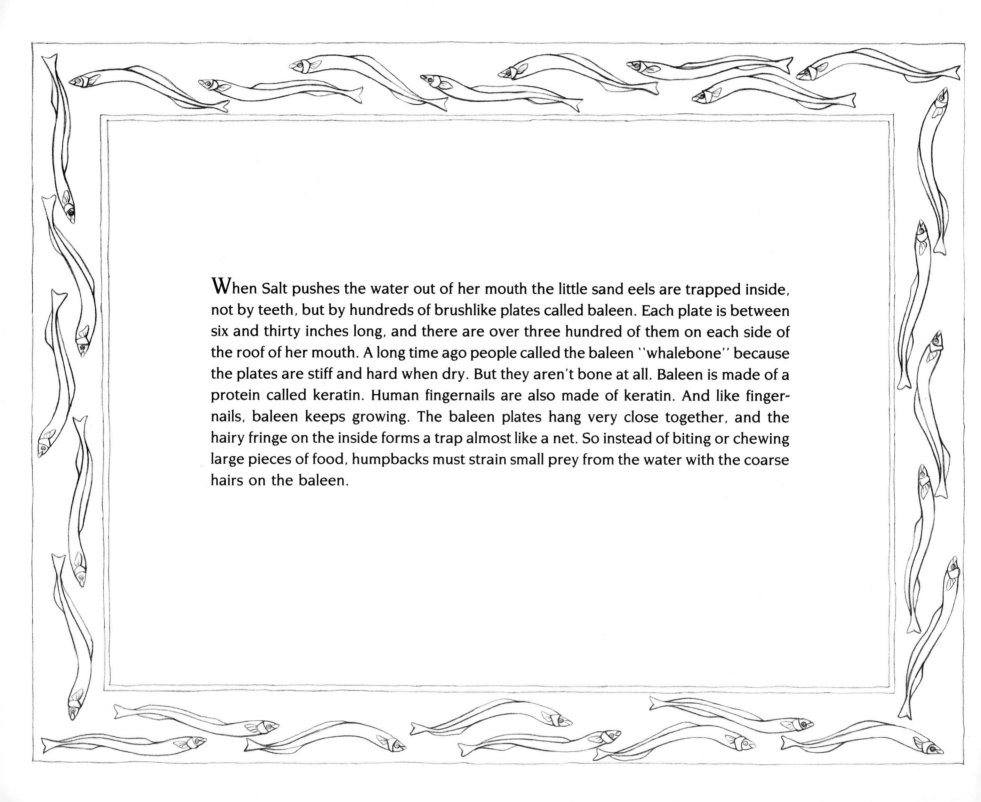

When Salt pushes the water out of her mouth the little sand eels are trapped inside, not by teeth, but by hundreds of brushlike plates called baleen. Each plate is between six and thirty inches long, and there are over three hundred of them on each side of the roof of her mouth. A long time ago people called the baleen ''whalebone'' because the plates are stiff and hard when dry. But they aren't bone at all. Baleen is made of a protein called keratin. Human fingernails are also made of keratin. And like fingernails, baleen keeps growing. The baleen plates hang very close together, and the hairy fringe on the inside forms a trap almost like a net. So instead of biting or chewing large pieces of food, humpbacks must strain small prey from the water with the coarse hairs on the baleen.

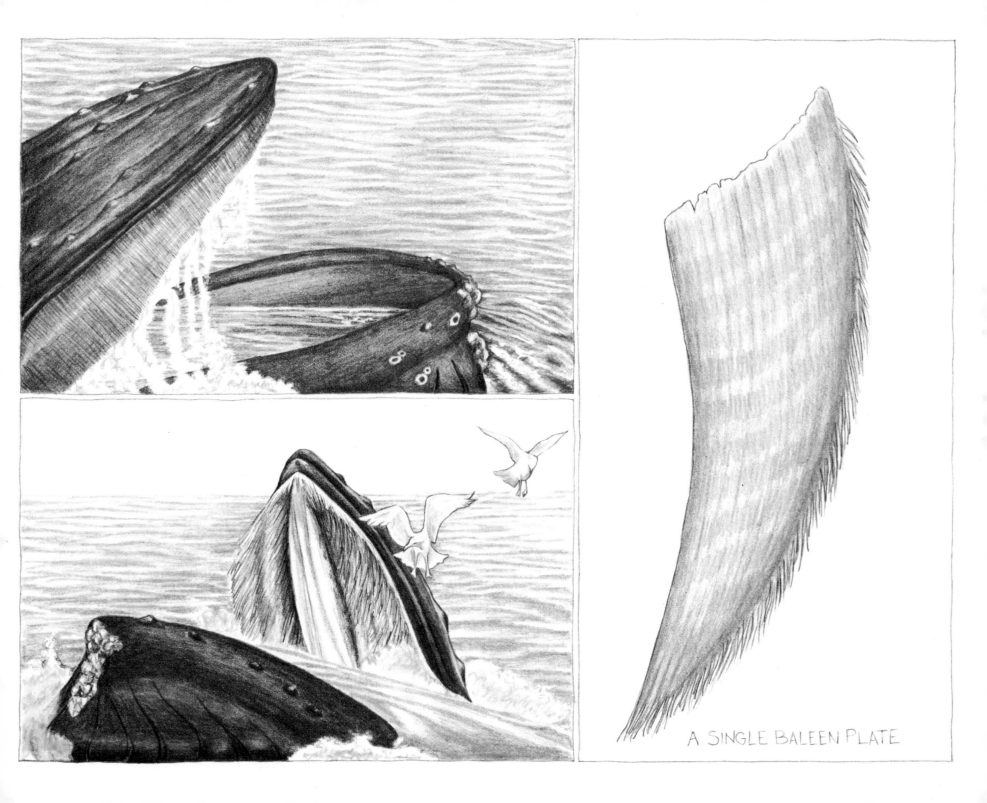

A SINGLE BALEEN PLATE

After a long winter down south with no food, Salt and all the other adult humpbacks arriving at Stellwagen are unbelievably hungry. Eating is their main activity all summer. Thousands of fish are needed to fill a humpback! Their stomachs may hold up to a ton of food, and these whales eat as much as three thousand pounds of fish (at least a million calories) each day during the summer months. They gain enormous amounts of weight as they build up a thick layer of blubber, or fat, which will help them live through the next winter without food.

One day while Salt is feeding nearby, Crystal suddenly swims right into a huge mass of bubbles. He is surrounded by light green froth and can't see where he's going! Twisting in small circles, Crystal flounders for a few seconds, then turns upward and splashes to the surface.

Salt comes up about twenty feet away and quickly dives again. Crystal watches as once more a large mass of air bubbles rises up through the water. They are coming from his mother! Seconds after the bubbles reach the surface, Salt comes up in the middle of the cloud of foam with her mouth wide open. Thousands of sand eels jump at the surface, rippling the water in a huge pool of little splashes. And birds—gulls, terns, gannets, petrels, shearwaters—dive and swoop low toward her. Some of the birds pick eels right out of the water with their beaks!

Again and again, Salt continues this bubble feeding. Some of the birds even land on her head and take a few steps, hitching a ride on Salt's back as she lunges at the surface. One brave gull flies right into Salt's open mouth to snatch a wriggling eel!

After his first experience with the bubbles, Crystal now stays safely out of the way. Maybe the bubbles help push those fast eels to the surface and group them together so Salt can get more in each mouthful. Or perhaps the bubbles hide Salt from the eels as she chases them.

In the weeks that follow Salt is often joined by ten or twelve, or even as many as twenty-five, other humpbacks. They feed together with incredible energy for a few

minutes, or even several hours. Some make bubble clouds and feed at the surface, while others catch their fish deep below. Land mammals would have to be careful that they didn't inhale water down their throats as they swallowed the fish, which would make them cough or drown. But whales' bodies have changed, and they no longer breathe through their mouths at all! The blowhole on top of their heads is connected directly to their lungs, and the lips of the blowhole are shut tight when the whales dive underwater.

Salt knows many of the animals because often the same humpbacks return to Stellwagen Bank each summer. Over two hundred humpbacks choose these waters to be their feeding ground each year. Probably many of the adults in this regular group first came here as calves with their mothers, just like Crystal. Now they return to the same feeding area that they first knew.

Only a few of the new calves from Silver Bank have come to Stellwagen this summer. The others have traveled with their mothers to other feeding areas farther north. But little Tanith is here with his mother, Nurse. Nurse was given her name because she was first seen in the company of an injured female whale named Silver.

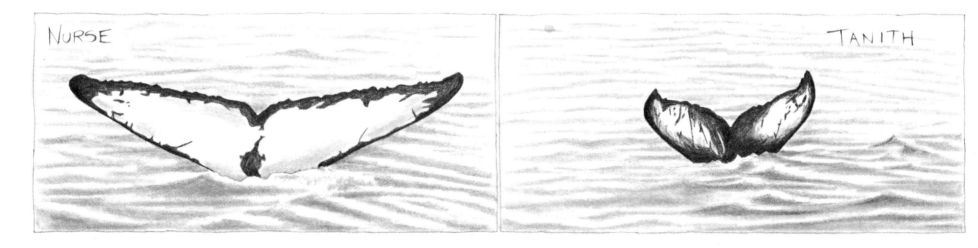

NURSE   TANITH

Beltane

Silver

Falco

Epaulet

This summer Silver is back too, with *her* calf, Beltane. Silver's tail certainly looks different from any other humpback's—part of it is gone! Some years ago she had an accident, most likely with a boat propeller, and half of her fluke was cut off. Even though this was a very serious injury, she recovered. Silver swims easily and is now a new mother.

Another calf is here with Crystal, Tanith, and Beltane. Her name is Epaulet, and her flukes are almost all black, just like those of her mother, Falco. Falco is one of the largest females here. She is about forty-three feet long, and her flippers are very dark for a humpback.

Stellwagen is a nursery for these young calves, as well as the feeding ground for their mothers and the other adults.

SUMMER

Humpbacks are not the only kind of whale that comes to Stellwagen Bank during the summer months. Crystal is probably very surprised when he first sees a whale almost twice as big as his mother—nearly seventy feet long, and a *very* fast swimmer. Fins, or finbacks, are the second largest type of whale in the world (only the giant blue whale is bigger). They are also among the fastest, which is why they are nicknamed "the greyhounds of the sea."

Finbacks look different from humpbacks. They are the only mammal known to have such uneven color on their bodies. The lower jaw and front baleen plates are white on the right side and black on the left. These color patterns are reversed inside the mouth and on the tongue. Their flippers are very short, and the dorsal fin is tall and sharply pointed. The finback's spout goes straight up, fifteen to twenty-five feet high, not low and bushy like a humpback's blow.

There are often several minke whales in the area, too. They are close to Crystal's size, only twenty to twenty-five feet long, and their spout is barely visible. Minkes have a distinct white band on their small flippers. Minke and finback whales do not have teeth either. Like the humpbacks, they strain their food through plates of baleen. They all come to Stellwagen to feed on the thousands of small fish and shrimp there.

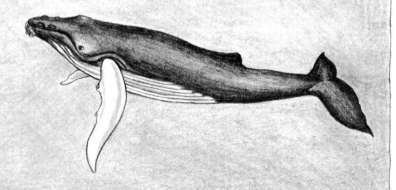

In July other visitors arrive as the water comes alive with activity, and Crystal finally sees a kind of whale that is *smaller* than he is! Actually he hears the dolphins before he sees them. It sounds like a chorus of squeaks and whistles, and in the distance are many little white splashes. Soon the group comes closer, the squeaks and whistles grow very loud, and Crystal gets a good look at the Atlantic white-sided dolphins!

Even though these dolphins are only six to eight feet long, they *are* whales. Unlike the other whales on Stellwagen Bank they have teeth, and all whales with teeth have only a single opening in their blowhole instead of two. The dolphins also enjoy feeding on the little sand eels, as well as the herring, smelt,

and squid in these waters. They don't slow down for Crystal, but keep up a very fast swim, whizzing by him on both sides and even underneath. Often they leap clear of the water. Unlike baleen whales, most toothed whales swim in tightly knit family groups, called pods. There are over a hundred dolphins in this group! The little dolphin calves stay right next to their mothers, swimming just as fast as the adults.

The sounds the dolphins make in the water help them ''see'' to find such things as food, land, and other dolphins. It's called echolocation. (The squeaks bounce off an object like an *echo*, and this helps the dolphins *locate*.) Within only a few minutes, their sounds begin to fade, and the splashes are once again in the distance.

Minkes, finbacks, dolphins, and humpbacks swim and feed together all summer on Stellwagen Bank. Many of these whales travel to other areas to feed sometimes, and one day in August Salt and Crystal venture away from the bank.

They swim north into very deep water, over six hundred feet. Crystal takes long dives into the dark, cooler water far below. Several miles farther north the ocean bottom rises up again into ledges with gaps and basins in between. This is called Jeffreys Ledge, another shallow area in the sea off the coasts of New Hampshire and Maine. Crystal swims more quickly to keep up with Salt, who is rapidly approaching a patch of murky red water. She lunges with her mouth open several times and moves away toward some other feeding humpbacks and out of Crystal's sight. The red in the water is from millions of tiny shrimp called krill, and Salt is enjoying a big meal of them.

Meanwhile, Crystal dives to the bottom and explores the seaweeds on the rocky ledges. Suddenly his flipper is snagged close to some rocks. He arches his back and feels a tight pull near his tail also. He can't get loose, and very soon he must swim back to the surface to breathe! Crystal rolls over and tries to push away from his invisible trap. After several twists and finally a violent thrust, he breaks free and rushes to the surface for air. A few minutes later he dives again and cautiously approaches the bottom. There he finds an old flag and buoy attached to some cord and a very thin, almost transparent net. It is a discarded gill net—the kind of net used to trap flounder, cod, and other fish—now a danger to all whales.

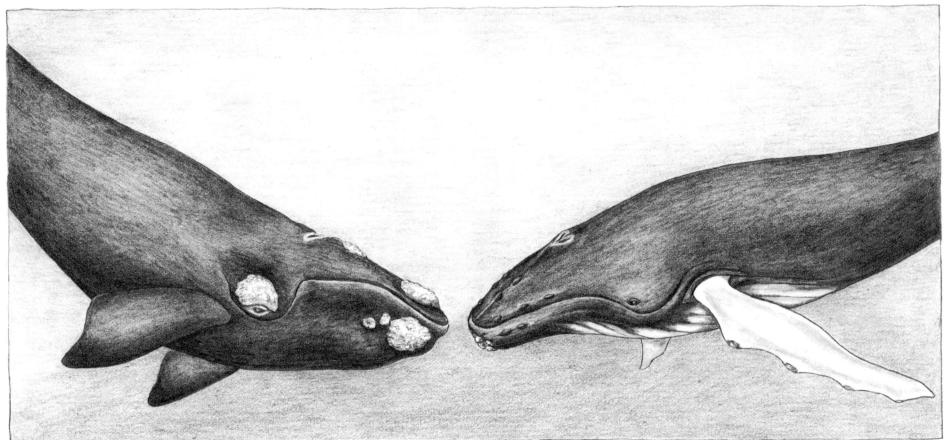

Suddenly a moving shape appears nearby. It is a whale calf, just Crystal's size. It is very strange looking! There is no dorsal fin on this little calf's back. Its fluke is triangle-shaped, pointed, and dark on both sides. The two openings in the blowhole are widely separated, so its spout comes out in a V shape. Strangest of all is the calf's funny looking head, which is covered with light-colored growths like warts around the blowhole and eyes, and along the lower jaw. It is a right whale calf!

The growths on the right whale's head are called callosities. Like baleen, they are made up of keratin. These growths are home to small creatures like barnacles and whale lice.

There are very few right whales left today because years ago many were hunted

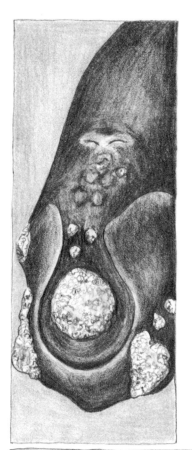

by humans. In those days, people used parts of the whales, like the baleen and oil, in their homes and work. These whales were especially easy to hunt because they are such slow swimmers and often come close to shore. Also they float after being killed. That's probably how they got their name—they were the "right" whales for the hunters.

For several minutes Crystal and the other calf swim in circles after one another. Then a very large right whale swims into view—the mother. She is bigger than Salt, about fifty-five feet long. Her calf joins her and they swim away. Perhaps they are traveling north to the Bay of Fundy, in Canada, where thirty to thirty-five other right whales feed during the summer.

Soon afterward Salt returns to Crystal's side and they head back toward Stellwagen Bank. Crystal never sees another right whale this summer.

Because there are so few right whales left they are now called an "endangered species." The humpbacks were also hunted and killed years ago, and they too are in danger of extinction. Both humpbacks and right whales are now protected from commercial hunting and can swim free with no fears—almost.

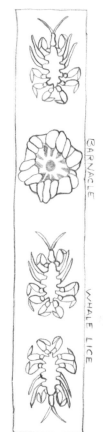

BARNACLE WHALE LICE

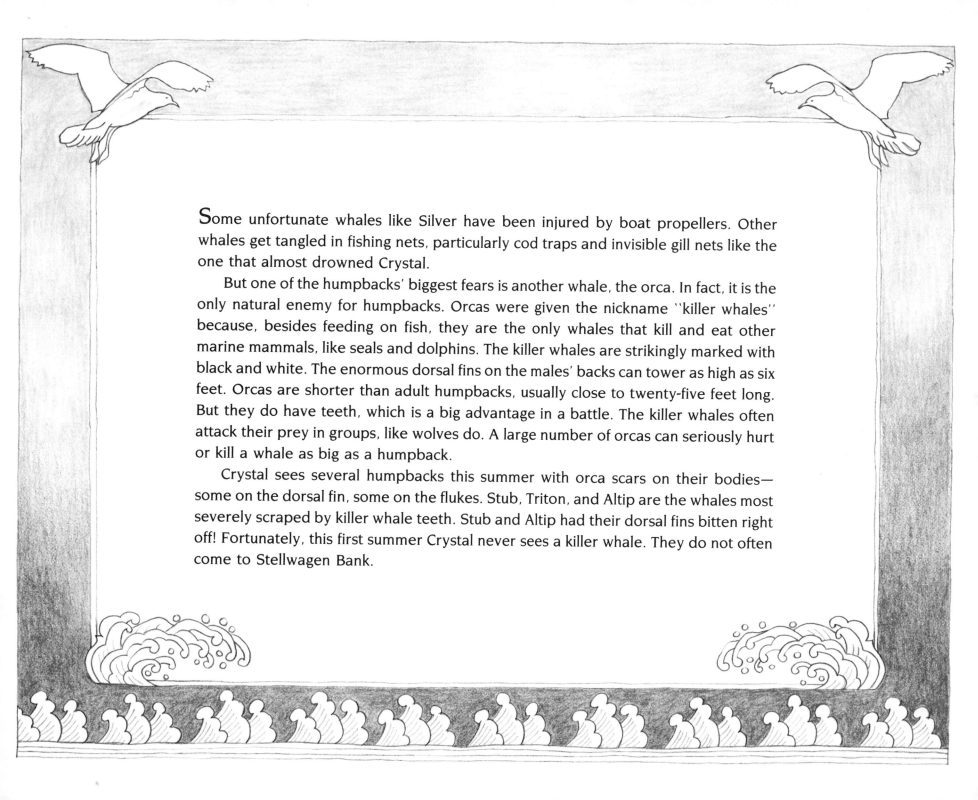

Some unfortunate whales like Silver have been injured by boat propellers. Other whales get tangled in fishing nets, particularly cod traps and invisible gill nets like the one that almost drowned Crystal.

But one of the humpbacks' biggest fears is another whale, the orca. In fact, it is the only natural enemy for humpbacks. Orcas were given the nickname ''killer whales'' because, besides feeding on fish, they are the only whales that kill and eat other marine mammals, like seals and dolphins. The killer whales are strikingly marked with black and white. The enormous dorsal fins on the males' backs can tower as high as six feet. Orcas are shorter than adult humpbacks, usually close to twenty-five feet long. But they do have teeth, which is a big advantage in a battle. The killer whales often attack their prey in groups, like wolves do. A large number of orcas can seriously hurt or kill a whale as big as a humpback.

Crystal sees several humpbacks this summer with orca scars on their bodies— some on the dorsal fin, some on the flukes. Stub, Triton, and Altip are the whales most severely scraped by killer whale teeth. Stub and Altip had their dorsal fins bitten right off! Fortunately, this first summer Crystal never sees a killer whale. They do not often come to Stellwagen Bank.

Besides whales, there are lots and lots of boats on the bank. Although most of them are there to fish, many of them are hunting for whales like Crystal—but not to kill. These vessels are filled with people who want only to see and photograph all the different kinds of whales. The whale-watching boats never come too close to the whales, especially if Crystal is nursing or logging with Salt. But sometimes the whales approach the boats! Crystal hears the motors long before the boats are nearby. The hum of the engines is a strange new sound that draws Crystal away from Salt to investigate. Time after time he leaves Salt's side and swims directly to the boats. Salt, always watchful, sometimes swims between Crystal and the boats and steers him away. Other times she follows, and together they circle the vessels and even swim underneath them. Perhaps they can hear the delighted cheers from the passengers.

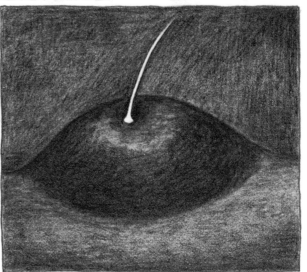

Even while close to the boats, Crystal is playful. He slaps his flippers and lobtails. Sometimes he hangs straight up and down in the water and slowly brings his head above the surface. This is called spyhopping. Even his eyes come out of the water! His bumpy chin rises several feet above the surface, exposing the barnacles that have attached themselves to his skin underneath. There are white circles there too, and these are scars where old barnacles have fallen off. Adult humpbacks sometimes have as much as a thousand pounds of three different species of barnacles stuck on their throats and flukes!

The bumps on the chin are another clue that whales are distantly related to land mammals. They still have hair! Those baseball-sized lumps in front of the blowhole and on the chin are tubercles. Many years ago sailors and whalers called them ''stovebolts'' because they thought the bumps held the head together, just like the bolts on an old cast-iron stove! Actually each knob is a large hair follicle with one or two hairs, or bristles, sticking out of each one. Maybe these hairs work like a cat's whiskers, helping the whale feel the movement of the water, or fish swimming by.

FALL

In September, after much practice, Crystal masters a very impressive breach. A breach is the most powerful single action performed by any animal—when a whale jumps partly or all the way out of the water and lands with an enormous splash! Crystal is nine months old and is no longer an awkward young calf. He is now as strong as his mother.

Humpbacks breach often, and in a number of different ways. Sometimes they tail breach, which is almost like doing a headstand as they thrust the lower half of their body out of the water. Other times they come out headfirst and land in a belly-flop several times in a row. Most often they come out headfirst and land on their backs or sides, sometimes turning in mid-air with their huge flippers outspread. At no other time do they look more like the "big-winged New Englander." When a full-grown humpback breaches, it has to lift thirty to thirty-five tons (over sixty thousand pounds) of whale into the air! Even though a leap like this must take an incredible amount of energy, some whales breach fifty or even a hundred times in a row!

All of these breaches create huge splashes and sprays that can be seen from a great distance. The breaches also make a lot of noise, and these sounds travel beneath the surface of the water five times faster than in air. Whales can hear each other jumping even if they're far apart, so this may be one way they keep in touch with one another. Breaching might also help knock some of the barnacles off their skin. There are many reasons why the whales might splash about with such energy, but for young whales like Crystal, it may be just great fun—and Salt often joins right in!

The water is becoming cooler now, and so is the air. On land the first frosts have come, and the trees are turning brilliant red, yellow, and orange. Soon it will snow. Salt has been feeding all summer and has probably gained a ton or more. Crystal has tasted his first sand eels too, and he continues to grow. Now he is nearly twenty-five feet long, double his size at birth!

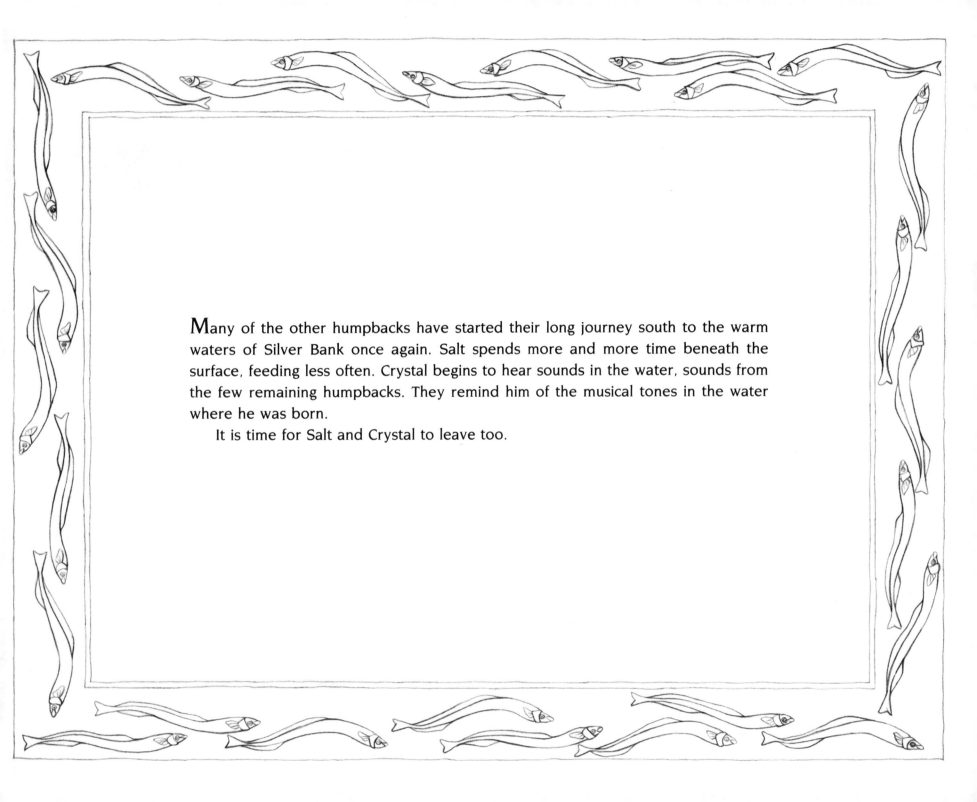

Many of the other humpbacks have started their long journey south to the warm waters of Silver Bank once again. Salt spends more and more time beneath the surface, feeding less often. Crystal begins to hear sounds in the water, sounds from the few remaining humpbacks. They remind him of the musical tones in the water where he was born.

It is time for Salt and Crystal to leave too.

In some ways the trip south is an easier swim for both of them. Now Crystal and Salt are well-fed and stronger, and Crystal doesn't have to nurse as often as he did during their trip north in the spring. Even so, it is a long journey, and the weather changes rapidly. The skies darken many times as heavy rains pound the ocean and beat upon their backs. Gusty winds sweep the seas into high swells and enormous breaking waves. Some days it is exhausting to swim against the waves, and they cover only a little distance. Salt and Crystal often hold their breath for as long as fifteen minutes as they swim beneath the surface as much as possible. They stay very close together. On clear, calm days with smooth seas they travel more easily and catch up on their rest by logging as long as necessary.

It is well into December before Salt and Crystal meet up with several humpback whales after swimming nearly sixteen hundred miles. Once again, at a time when much of the northern hemisphere is cold and icy, these whales are swimming into the warm waters of Silver Bank. And the water is filled with songs—the same sounds Crystal heard last year.

Like dolphins, the humpbacks are able to make an endless variety of sounds, including the highest and lowest notes that humans are able to hear. There are moans and groans, snores, grunts, thumps, clicks, chirps, cries, and even whistles coming from these huge whales. Sometimes these sounds come out in patterns, with different phrases and themes repeating over and over just like songs. These songs welcome the returning whales. The singers are adult males. They do not swim, but hang very still beneath the surface when they make their songs.

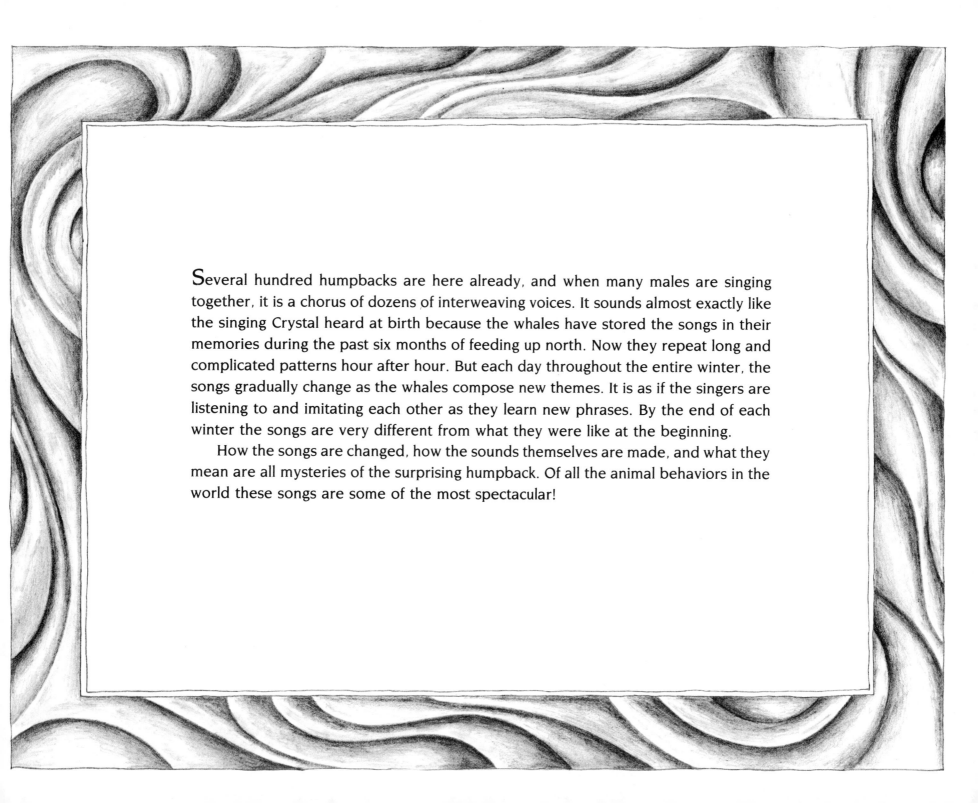

Several hundred humpbacks are here already, and when many males are singing together, it is a chorus of dozens of interweaving voices. It sounds almost exactly like the singing Crystal heard at birth because the whales have stored the songs in their memories during the past six months of feeding up north. Now they repeat long and complicated patterns hour after hour. But each day throughout the entire winter, the songs gradually change as the whales compose new themes. It is as if the singers are listening to and imitating each other as they learn new phrases. By the end of each winter the songs are very different from what they were like at the beginning.

How the songs are changed, how the sounds themselves are made, and what they mean are all mysteries of the surprising humpback. Of all the animal behaviors in the world these songs are some of the most spectacular!

This is all so familiar to Crystal now. A year is over, and he is right back where he began. By January several new calves are born, and soon the warm water is as crowded and active as last winter.

Most young humpbacks leave their mothers after they are about a year old. It is likely that Crystal will leave Salt soon and spend more of his time with other whales closer to his age. Probably Crystal will return north to Stellwagen Bank in the spring next year to feed. This time he will make the trip all on his own. At Stellwagen he may occasionally see his mother again, as well as his old friends Tanith, Beltane, Epaulet, and all the other whales who feed together there.

Maybe Salt will become pregnant again next year and Crystal will later have a new brother or sister.

In a few more years, when Crystal journeys south to Silver Bank once again, he will be singing a song of his own.

Crystal's adventures have only just begun!

EPILOGUE

The discovery that fluke patterns are like fingerprints quickly expanded humpback research. Over three thousand humpback whales have now been identified in the northwest Atlantic, thanks to the contributions of researchers working in the waters as far north as Greenland and all the way south to the West Indies. Photographs of the whales' individual flukes fill a bulging catalogue that is continually expanding.

These photographs are like a natural tagging system. Now particular whales can be recognized and observed several times each season, not only in their northern feeding grounds, but in the warm southern waters as well. As these sightings are repeated year after year, exciting clues have been revealed about the whales' lives: where they migrate, how and what they eat, how often they have calves, the possible reasons for the sounds and songs they make.

In 1976 the first humpback whale in the Gulf of Maine was named by Dr. Charles ''Stormy'' Mayo, of the Provincetown Center for Coastal Studies. That whale was Salt. Giving names to these whales has now become an organized group effort, with a naming party held each spring in Provincetown. Researchers vote on names for the new whales and calves of the previous year. They try to find a name that suggests a certain physical mark on the whale, such as Scratch or Speckles. With so many hump-

backs now being studied it would be difficult to remember a particular whale by a computer code or catalogue number like #0036 (Salt). The names make it easier for researchers from different areas to compare their sightings.

Crystal was first seen as a young calf with Salt in 1980, and he has been resighted regularly on Stellwagen Bank over the years, as well as on Silver Bank in 1982. Hundreds of photographs and hours of video record his delightful behaviors as a calf, and he has remained a favorite, along with Salt and the other 1980 calves and mothers. All of these "families" have grown, and Crystal now has four siblings. Salt was seen with new calves in 1983, 1985, 1987 and 1989.

Crystal's "brother," born in 1987 and named Brine (salty water), was briefly entangled in fishing lines in an incident similar to Crystal's mishap in this book. On August 8, 1989, two-year-old Brine was feeding on the northwest corner of Stellwagen Bank when he swam into an anchor line from a tuna fishing boat. The line became stuck in his baleen, and when he thrashed to get loose, the line and anchor chain wrapped around his tail. In a few hours the crew of the tuna boat and naturalists from local whale-watching boats were able to free him.

Falco was seen with her second known calf in 1984, and her third in 1986. Both

Nurse and Silver had calves in 1983 and again in 1985. Each has since brought back another calf, Silver in 1988 and Nurse in 1989. Beltane, born the same year as Crystal, became a mother in 1985. She was the first identified female calf to have a calf of her own, making her mother, Silver, the first documented grandmother.

Sadly, Beltane is no longer with us. Her body was discovered on a beach on Cape Cod on November 28, 1987. She was one of at least fourteen humpback whales who died after feeding on mackerel that were infected with a poisonous biotoxin. Beltane was a very special whale – the first humpback in the world to have been followed from birth until she had her first calf, and we learned a lot from her.

The relatively new field of cetacean (whale) research continues to grow each year. The great whales, including the humpbacks, cannot be kept in captivity. We see only what they allow us to see, and many of their activities remain a mystery. As a few questions are answered, dozens more are asked and new theories are offered. The work continues in the hope that we will one day understand, to what small degree might be possible, the lives and deaths of these largest of all mammals.

The increase in public whale watching cruises has been helpful to research because many of these guides on these trips are gathering valuable information on a

daily basis. And the first-hand experience of observing these whales in their natural surroundings has made thousands and thousands of passengers aware of how very fragile the whales' world is – and their world is, of course, part of the same ecosystem on which we all depend. The future of their ocean environment will be most greatly affected by people.

After a long and frustrating struggle, the end of commercial whale hunting may soon be in sight. But even if whaling ceases, pollution of the ocean can still tragically upset the food chain. This can change and even kill many species of plants and fish, which in turn affects the lives of marine mammals.

Another problem of increasing importance is entanglement: whales getting caught in fishing nets, resulting in severe injury or death. From 1975 through 1988, the National Marine Fisheries Service was notified of twenty-seven cases where whales were found entangled in ropes or nets on Jeffreys Ledge and in Massachusetts Bay. No doubt there were even more cases that were never discovered and reported. Newspapers all over the United States brought attention to this problem in October 1984 when a young female humpback named Ibis was seriously entangled in a gill net close to the coast of Massachusetts. The situation was dangerous for the rescuers, and

appeared hopeless, yet two brave and risky attempts to cut off the net were finally successful. The release of Ibis had been called impossible, and is now often called a miracle. Not all whales can be so fortunate.

Awareness is the first step in preventing these problems, and awareness is increasing at a rewarding pace. It is also happening earlier — with children. And it is to the children that this story of Crystal is offered, as well as to their parents.

We all have so much to learn.

To quote Katy Payne, who, with Dr. Roger Payne, was one of the pioneers in unlocking some of the mysteries of the humpbacks' songs:

When the guns stopped.
We started to hear singing.

SUGGESTED READING

Bank St. College of Education. *Voyage of the Mimi*. New York: Holt, Rinehart and Winston, 1984.

Earle, Sylvia A. ''Humpbacks: The Gentle Whales.'' *National Geographic* 155 (January 1979).

Gardner, Robert. *The Whale Watcher's Guide*. New York: Julian Messner, 1984.

Garrett, Howard, and Candice Keays. *New England Whales*. Gloucester, Mass.: Cape Ann Publishing Co., 1985.

Gibbs, Jane M. *Whales Off New England*. Newbury, Mass.: Gibbs and Gibbs, 1982.

Katona, Steven K., Valerie Rough, and David T. Richardson. *A Field Guide of Whales, Porpoises, and Seals of the Gulf of Maine and Eastern Canada*. New York: Scribner's, 1983.

Nicklin, Flip, and Roger Payne. ''New Light on the Singing Whales.'' *National Geographic* 161 (April 1982).

Payne, Roger. ''Humpbacks: Their Mysterious Songs.'' *National Geographic* 155 (January 1979).

Weinrich, Mason T. *Observations: The Humpback Whales of Stellwagen Bank*. Gloucester, Mass: Whale Research Press, 1983.

Winn, Lois King, and Howard E. Winn. *Wings in the Sea: The Humpback Whale*. Hanover and London: University Press of New England, 1985.